POWERFUL PANELS

A STEP-BY-STEP GUIDE TO MODERATING LIVELY & INFORMATIVE PANEL DISCUSSIONS AT MEETINGS, CONFERENCES & CONVENTIONS

KRISTIN ARNOLD

QPC Press
Scottsdale, AZ

Also by Kristin Arnold

Boring to Bravo
Proven Presentation Techniques to Engage, Involve and Inspire Your Audiences to Action

Team Basics
Practical Strategies for Team Success

Email Basics
Practical Tips to Improve Team Communication

Team Energizers
50 Practical Team Activities

**Powerful Panels: How to Moderate a Lively and Informative Panel Discussion
at Meetings, Conferences and Conventions**

Copyright © 2013 by Kristin J. Arnold
Published by QPC Press, www.QPCpress.com
11890 E Juan Tabo Road, Scottsdale, AZ, 800.589.4733

Printed in the United States of America
Library of Congress Catalog Number:
ISBN: 978-0-9676313-6-3

Introduction

Congratulations! You have been asked to moderate a panel discussion at your organization's meeting, conference or convention. **This could be a great opportunity for you to become more visible within your organization and beyond.** You were honored to be asked, so you said, "Yes, of course I'll do that!"

Panels are famous for being the either the best part of the program – or for being the worst.

In a recent survey of over 400 meeting professionals, they said that 50% of the panels were merely "okay" – largely because of issues with the moderator. Unfortunately, many moderators simply wing it. After all, how hard can it be to ask a few people some questions and then do some audience Q&A?

Truth be told, it's not hard once you know how. Most of your work is done BEFORE the panel steps on stage. **When you follow this step-by-step guide, the panel discussion will flow. Your panelists will look brilliant and you'll be the hero.**

This book was written for you, the first-time panelist; however, seasoned moderators find it to be a useful resource as well. It's a simple how-to guide to make sure you moderate a lively, engaging and informative panel discussion. **Simply follow this five-step process and, in no time at all, you will have the knowledge and the confidence to moderate a lively and informative panel discussion.**

Table of Contents

What is a Panel?

A panel discussion is a specific format used in a meeting, conference or convention. It is a live or virtual discussion about a specific topic amongst a selected group of panelists who share differing perspectives in front of a large audience.

The panel is typically facilitated by a "moderator" who guides the panel and the audience through the event.

The panel, typically 3-4 experts or practitioners in the field, shares facts, offers opinions and responds to audience questions either through questions curated by the moderator or taken from the audience directly.

The panel session typically lasts for 60-90 minutes.

The best panels feel like a fast-paced, unpredictable conversation between smart people on stage and smart people in the audience.

Scott Kirsner
Journalist, Panel Moderator
Conference Organizer

Panel Formats

For a one hour panel, there are a few popular formats:

Q&A Style. A 2-5 minute introduction of the topic and panelists, 25 minutes of curated questions from the moderator, 25 minutes of audience questions ending with a summary and thanks.

Initial Remarks Style. A 2-5 minute introduction of the topic with each panelist taking 5 minutes to introduce themselves and their perspectives on the topic. Then 20 minutes of curated questions from the moderator, 10-15 minutes of Q&A with the audience ending with a summary and thanks.

Presentation Style. A 2-5 minute introduction of the topic and panelists. Each panelist has 10-15 minutes of uninterrupted sharing of his or her perspective, 5-10 minutes of Q&A ending with a summary and thanks.

There are specialty formats (largely derived from television shows) as well:

- Debate (political or otherwise)
- Point/Counterpoint (60 Minutes)
- McLaughlin Group
- Hot Seats (American Idol, X Factor and The Voice are examples)
- Café Style (Friends)

A Panel is NOT…

A *set of presentations*, one after another. The panel format allows for a brief introduction and then discussion among the panelists and audience. If the majority of the panel agenda is centered around presenting information, then just give each panelist a speaking slot with a Q&A after each speaker.

A *one-on-one interview* with each panelist. Many untrained moderators simply ask questions of each panelist, one after another, rather than build the dialogue into a conversation. Unless there is interplay among the panelists, have an "up close and personal" interview with each speaker.

Just Q&A from the audience. When the focus is completely on answering the audience's questions, you have a forum or "town hall" meeting.

Not that any of these formats are bad; they are different than and an alternative to a panel discussion. Just call it like you see it, be it a panel, presentation, interview or forum.

Use a panel when you believe the group of panelists will generate something more interesting than any one individual panel member could generate on his/her own.

The Panel Moderator

As the moderator, your job is to help the audience get their needs met through a panel format. You set the tone, the pace and control the content, staying ever-vigilant in keeping it relevant for the audience. It is your responsibility to make sure the panel is lively, engaging and worthwhile. The success (or failure) of the program rests largely in your hands.

Depending on the panel objectives, the panel moderator, has several roles and responsibilities:

Champion for the Audience. Makes sure the panel is talking about timely issues that the audience cares about. Continually assesses and reacts to the audience, keeping the conversation on track and meaningful for them.

Facilitator. Sets the agenda, keeps the discussions on track, brings out differing opinions and the most interesting information, balances panelist participation, clarifies any confusion and intervenes as needed – especially when someone is dominating the conversation.

Timekeeper. Makes sure the panel starts and ends on time and follows the time frames on the agenda. Makes sure they don't spend too much or too little time on any one single element.

Logistician. Makes sure the panelists show up on time, the room is set, microphones are working, etc.

Instigator. Probes beneath the surface, asking tough questions of the panel, building the dialogue, keeping the conversation lively and getting out of the way when the conversation is going well. Pushes the panelists to talk about specifics rather than speak in generalities. Gets the dialogue going with the audience and sustains the conversation in order to get their questions answered.

Knowledgeable. Knows enough about the topic, terms, key issues and acronyms to guide the conversation and ask thoughtful questions.

Content Coordinator. Works with the panelists to make sure their presentations do not overlap. Identifies the areas of debate and controversy. Coordinates slideshows where appropriate.

Energizer. Models energy and enthusiasm. Works the room and engages the audience. Injects a little humor where appropriate to keep it lively.

Neutral & Objective. Withholds own personal opinions and judgment. Doesn't show bias or favoritism toward any particular side, faction or person.

The Moderator as a Content Contributor

Obviously, everyone has an opinion. But if you have a lot to say about the topic, then you should be a *panelist* and not the moderator. Moderators who have deep expertise and opinions on the topic will want to jump in – maybe more frequently than they should – and then who facilitates the moderator?

For some specific formats (e.g., Hot Seat), the moderator *may* be expected to participate as well. It's not easy to combine the role of moderator and expert as they may end up dominating the discussion and hog the show!

There are times, however, where it *may* be appropriate for the moderator to add his/her own opinion and perspective to the conversation.

Here are some examples:

- Opening remarks on the topic (in a balanced way) before formally posing the issue to the panelists.

- Transitions between the last question and the next one.

- When the question has not been adequately answered. If you have given the panelists the opportunity to answer and you get nothing or you have something *significant* to add, make your contribution at the end of the conversation.

The moderator should make everyone else look smart while providing tremendous value to the audience. When it comes to contributing content, the moderator is the fallback, just in case.

Just as an excellent party requires an overall theme, marvelous guests and careful planning before the party can start, so does an excellent panel discussion. Follow this 5-step process to make sure your panel discussion is the highlight of the entire event!

Even at this point early in the planning phase, several decisions have already been made by the meeting chair and/or planner, so you need to come up to speed on what has already been decided and what assumptions have been made for you. When you clarify the starting conditions, you will find that you have much more freedom than you initially thought!

Have a chat with the meeting chair and/or planner to discuss:

The Event. The panel discussion is typically one session within an entire event. Determine where you are in the event agenda, what comes before and after the panel discussion. Take a look at the event website and marketing materials.

Panel Dates/Time/Location. Block this day off on your schedule and plan to get to the venue well ahead of the start time.

Panel Title. An intriguing title will capture your audience's attention. Work with the meeting chair to develop a catchy and effective title that is consistent with the event theme.

Panel Objectives. Clarify the stated objectives for the panel – especially if marketing material has already been published. What do you want them to know, think or feel about the topic?

Panel Format. Discuss their vision for the panel. How formal or informal? Traditional or more unique? Confirm how much latitude you have to play with the format and agenda.

Sponsoring Organization. Review the mission of the business, association or organization. Ask about their past experiences of having panels on their program – the good, the bad and the ugly.

Audience. Confirm the audience size, demographics and expectations for the panel discussion.

- What's the expected level of expertise in the room around the panel topic?

- What are their key interests, needs and concerns?

- What questions are they hoping to find answers to?

- What will be the impact of the panelists' comments on their work and lives?

Panelists. Get the name, bio and contact information for any panelist who has already been invited or confirmed to participate, why they were selected, as well as a copy of what has been communicated to them. Ask for recommendations *(see Step 2)*. Determine any inducements you can offer additional panelists to serve and if there are any promotional policies or prohibitions you need to be aware of.

Bonus: Panel Planning Worksheet

Go online to download a comprehensive worksheet to capture the starting conditions while talking to the meeting chair and/or planner.

www.PowerfulPanels.com

Success Criteria. Ask about who and how they will determine and evaluate the success of the panel. Evaluation forms? Hallway buzz?

Room Logistics. Find out about the room size and layout, furniture setup and color of the backdrop.

Audio/Visual. Determine the availability of audio (microphones), visual (video projection) and internet (Wi-Fi) connectivity.

Rights. Ask if panel will be recorded (audio and/or video) or live streamed? If so, ask for the release form the moderator and panel needs to sign.

Support Staff. Ask about any additional support you will have in the room, e.g., room monitors, microphone runners, etc.

Promotion. Offer to help get the word out (see page 14).

Attire. Determine the expected attire/dress for the conference.

The conference organizers may have already invited the panelists. If so, you'll have to work with what you have. Otherwise, you'll need to round up a handful of interesting people with different experiences and perspectives.

What's a "handful?" It depends on the situation, but for most panels, 3-4 experts is perfect. Any fewer and it becomes difficult to flesh out all the points of view or simply becomes an interview. Five or more becomes unwieldy where panelists compete for airtime.

The ideal panelist should have most, if not all of these traits:

Expertise. A recognized authority, newsmaker or thought leader within the industry who possesses strong enough credentials that generate credibility quickly through a bio or 30 second introduction. If you've got a lot to say about the topic, you might want to think about *being on* the panel rather than *moderating* it.

Practitioner. Maybe they aren't the most well known, but they actually have firsthand knowledge about the topic and have applied it successfully (or not) in the real world.

Stakeholders. Representatives along the value chain are also strong choices. Invite a high-profile end-user customer, an employee or representatives from your vendor-partners.

Dynamic. Panelists should be good conversationalists. How are they on the phone? Was it a monologue or a discussion? Review video footage to make sure the potential panelist has the ability to keep the audience engaged and interested.

Tailored. Some high profile personalities have one speech and won't (or cannot) tailor their presentation and/or comments for your specific audience and topic. Find someone who will.

Opinionated. A great panelist is willing to be opinionated and take a controversial position on a topic – without being a jerk.

Diverse. Beware of lining up a panel that is too similar and/or comfortable with each other. A group who is in complete agreement makes for a boring panel. A panel who knows each other well may lack a fresh perspective. A panel who looks too homogenous lacks visual diversity.

Invite and Confirm. Assemble a list of names, email addresses and direct or mobile phone numbers. As soon as possible, send an email with the date, time and location of the session and confirm their participation. Request their most up to date:

- Bio (Don't depend on their bio on their website – it's probably not current!)
- Twitter username
- Photo
- Audio-visual release form

Finally, be prepared for Murphy's Law: Anything can happen. Prepare a few backup panelists – just in case one cancels or doesn't show.

Aim High!

If you don't ask the people you really want to have on the panel, they can't say "yes."

Put yourself in the audience's shoes. Who would they want to hear? Ask the meeting chair or organizational "heavy hitters" – those who are are very visible, well-known and respected within the audience – who you should ask.

Invite the featured keynote speaker to be part of the panel discussion.

Google the "newsmakers" and invite them to participate either directly or ask someone in your network who knows them to invite them.

Look at your network and ask people you respect and admire to participate. Industry analysts, bloggers and journalists are good choices. Put out a call for panelists on your social networks.

Here are some ways to "sweeten the pot" to get them to say yes:

- Book signing
- Professional videotaping of the panel session
- Media mentions
- Extra press-only session
- Meet the panelists reception/dinner
- VIP private dinner
- Ability to share a case study about how their customers have been successful

The difference between a mediocre panel and an amazing panel discussion is in the preparation. The adage, "an ounce of prevention is worth a pound of cure" is distinctly true when it comes to panel discussions.

You will need to:

❑ Research your topic, panelists and audience
❑ Create the panel format, agenda and ground rules
❑ Write the welcome and introductions
❑ Curate the questions
❑ Decide the Q&A format
❑ Determine the logistics
❑ Confirm details with the panelists
❑ Assemble the slideshow
❑ Spread the word

Research Audience Expectations.

- *In Their Shoes.* Imagine the types of people (even specific individuals as a model) who are likely to attend. Preemptively ask some of the questions they are likely to ask.

- *Interview.* Ask the conference organizer for the names and contact information for three "influencers" or "heavy hitters" who may be in the audience. Ask them what they would like to hear about and what challenges they are facing.

- *Social Media.* Use the conference website, a blog post, Twitter or other feedback tool to glean questions from the community. Ask them to submit their most pressing issues and challenges.

- *Email or Voice Mail Blast.* Some organizations have the ability to blast a voice mail or email to all the participants encouraging them to attend the session and submit their questions.

Research the Topic, Panelists & Audience

It is your job to facilitate the conversation so the audience receives tremendous value from their expertise and perspectives. You cannot do this effectively if you don't know the people on your panel, the topic or what your audience expects.

Research the Topic. You don't need to be an expert, but you should have a working knowledge of the topic, terms, acronyms, key issues, challenges and perspectives to guide the conversation and ask thoughtful and insightful questions.

Research the Panelists. Google their work and views they hold on the topic. Review the panelists' websites, social profiles, books, reviews, bios, blogs, recent presentations, media mentions, papers, etc.

Take Notes. You don't need to know *everything* about the panelists' lives, but you should have a basic idea of their points of view on the topic. This will make it much easier to connect with and introduce each panelist.

WARNING: This research should take at least several hours – or more if you get sucked into the Google vortex!

Talk to Each Panelist either by phone or face to face and discuss:

- *Expectations.* Let them know what to expect (go over the format) and then ask them about their experiences with panels.

- *Content.* Given the topic, ask them what they would like to talk about. Tease out the juicy bits from the audience's point of view. Look for possible areas of contention with the other panelists' points of view.

- *Rapport.* As you talk to each of the panelists, you are not only assessing their speaking strengths, style and perspectives, but you are also creating a connection and building trust.

Generate a Draft List of Questions. As a result of all this research, compile a list of potentially provocative questions. These questions should be insightful and specifically:

- Tied to the topic

- Reflective of a specific panelist's work or interests

- Representative of issues the audience will be interested in

At this point, prepare more questions than you think you'll need – and make sure they cover the topical landscape.

Create the Panel Format

Once you have confirmed the starting conditions, panel objectives and done a bit of research, it is time to create the panel format.

Select the Panel Format. The typical panel consists of seven elements:

1. Welcome

2. Panelist introductions

3. Panelist presentations

4. Moderator-curated questions directed to the panelists

5. Questions from the audience directed to a panelist(s)

6. Summary

7. Thank you/administrative remarks

You may opt to do all seven, omit some or even create your own unique format. No format is perfect, so adjust the format to meet your objectives.

For a one hour panel, there are a few popular formats to consider *(see page 2)*:

- Q&A Style

- Initial Remarks Style

- Presentation Style

Consider a specialty format, largely derived from television shows):

- Debate (political or otherwise)

- Point/Counterpoint (60 Minutes)

- McLaughlin Group

- Hot Seats (American Idol, X Factor, The Voice are examples)

- Café Style (Friends).

Common Panel Formats

W/I	MC	Q&A	S/T

Q&A Style

W	I/P	I/P	I/P	I/P	MC	Q&A	S/T

Initial Remarks Style

W/I	P	P	P	P	Q&A	S/T

Presentation Style

Create an Agenda. Once you have selected the format, create a high-level agenda *with specific time frames.* Here's an example of a Q&A Style Panel Agenda:

0:00 Welcome, Format Overview, Agenda and Ground Rules

0:02 Brief Introduction of each panelist

0:05 Moderator-curated questions directed to the panelists

0:30 Questions from the audience directed to a panelist(s)

0:55 Summary

0:59 Thank you/administrative directions (where to go next, instructions for the book signing)

1:00 Adjourn

Preventions. During your research, you were alerted to a few things that you need to watch for or that could go wrong.

By creating some ground rules, you will be able to maintain control while encouraging a robust discussion.

Here are some examples of ground rules for the panelists to follow:

- Be additive. If you agree, say so if you must and move on.

- Not everyone needs to answer every question.

- Keep your answers crisp and concise. Save the long back story for the bar.

- Jump in if you have something new to say.

- One person talks at a time.

- Generate light and not heat. Let's have a healthy debate.

- No shameless promotion.

Write the Welcome

The welcoming comments and panel introductions are to connect the audience with the topic and the panelists – so the audience understands what's being proposed, who the panelists are and why they should listen to them.

Because these starting comments are so important, write out your talking points and/or script your welcome and introductions. Practice them so you are comfortable enough with the content and won't have to read it word for word.

Kick Off. Write your welcome, introduction and purpose. Lead into the topic with a short, interesting fact, statistic, quotation, anecdote or poll. Set the table by quickly giving an overview of why this topic is important now and what you hope to accomplish.

Process. Provide a high level review of the process as well as any ground rules. Encourage the attendees to submit their questions as you go, periodically or at a dedicated time (*See page 10*).

Your Role. Write your own brief introduction and clarify your role as the moderator. If you are also contributing content as a fellow panelist, say so at the onset.

Panelist Introductions.
Introductions should be brief, informative, professional and warm with a similar length and style.

- Have the panelists write their own introductions and send it to you for review and edits. Or,

- You write the introductions and send to the panelists for concurrence.

Controversy: Who Introduces the Panelists?

There is a great debate in the moderator community about who should introduce the panelists. While there is no "right way," you should be aware of the pro's and con's to each option:

Moderator Introduces. You are able to focus on the essential tidbits of information the audience needs to know to engage quickly into the conversation. An added benefit is that it allows you to control the clock. At least in the first five minutes, you won't already be behind schedule!

If you are introducing the panelists, create a two sentence bio for each panelist that quickly establishes why that person is uniquely qualified to be there. You may want to include an interesting comment on the position he is taking, why she is so passionate about the topic or why he was selected to be on the panel.

Panelist Introduces. It allows each panelist to loosen up and connect with the crowd. It allows each panelists to have a guaranteed amount of airtime. Unfortunately, it also allows the panelists to set the tone for the panel. They could be boring and go over time; then you are already in the hole before the discussion even starts!

No One Introduces! If you believe that everyone on the panel is already well known to the audience, consider skipping the introductions. Put up a summary slide and get down to business!

Seating. Decide how and when the panelists will be seated.

- Begin the session with all the panelists seated in their chairs

  OR

- Panelists come onto the stage and are seated as they are introduced.

Seat the panelists in the same order as you introduce them from left to right.

Seating Order. Pay particular attention to who speaks first as this sets the tone for the conversation. Select a panelist who is poised, well-structured and articulate. Or, if you want the panel to be a little irreverent, pick the most irreverent panelist to start!

The last panelist may summarize or define the differing positions, so select a panelist who is thoughtful, sees the big picture and won't get stuck in the minutia of the discussion.

If you have a "celebrity" who might intimidate or outshine the other panelists, consider placing the celebrity as the final panelist.

Curate the Questions

When preparing your questions, put yourself in your audience's shoes. Ask the questions that are on everyone's mind.

Get Your List. Pull out that long list of potential questions from your research.

- What's the most prevalent question on everyone's mind?

- Why is this topic important right now?

- What are the key challenges the audience is facing about this topic?

- What are the two things that are most important to share/discover on this topic during the panel?

- Where does the panel agree and disagree about the topic?

Cull Your List. Whittle your list down to at least two main questions per panelist. Keep a backup of ten or more questions to use if needed.

Sequence the Questions. Typically, moderator-curated questions have a flow that moves from strategic to the more tactical.

- *Strategic.* Start with broad or "high altitude" questions designed to discuss what is happening in the world.

- *Benefits.* Move to the benefits and/or consequences about why the audience should care.

- *Specifics.* Ask more specific questions where the panelists will be more inclined to share anecdotes or concrete examples.

- *Application.* Make sure the audience walks away with substantial value and the ability to apply the information.

Hot Potato or Ping Pong?

The first question should be designed to include some aspect of the title of the session and provide value for the audience at the same time. The first question sets the tone and lets the audience know how each panelist is going to contribute to the conversation. You have two strategies to start the moderator-curated questions:

Hot Potato. Ask the same question to each of the panelists. (You-Panelist 1-Panelist 2-Panelist 3).

Ping Pong. Ask a different question to each of the panelists. (You-Panelist 1-You-Panelist 2-You Panelist 3). Tailor this first question to highlight some specific aspect of the panelist's background. Just make sure you have the same level question (softie or hardball, but not both) for everyone else on the panel.

There are three schools of thought on the way you should start with moderator-curated questions:

1. *Softie.* Warm up the panelists with broad, easy questions so the panelists can settle in and relax. Ask for a definition, talk about the history of the topic or why this topic is so interesting. Then raise the stakes, probing into more controversial areas.

2. *Hardball.* Start out with a strong, provocative question. For example, ask each panelist, in 30 seconds or less to offer a strong opinion on the topic.

3. *Gauge the Room.* When the audience's skill level is not known, do some level-setting of the audience's experience. For example, ask for a show of hands, "How many people have less than 2 years experience writing Java? Between 2-5 years? And those who think they should be on the panel rather than out in the audience?"

Tweak the Questions. Rephrase the questions more economically (the shorter, the better) in order to position the question for the panelist and audience and to focus them to keep the panelists on track.

Bonus: Index Card Template

You may want to write the panelist intro and questions on an index card for you to access easily.

Consider using a key ring to keep the index cards in order during the session.

www.PowerfulPanels.com

Decide the Q&A Format

Questions from the audience can enrich the discussion or derail it, so decide ahead of time when and how you will manage questions.

When. There is no law that says you have to save your Q&A until the end. You can:

- *Take Questions As You Go.* Allow questions to percolate from the audience at any time.

- *Stop Periodically and Ask For Questions.* For example, stop for questions after each panelist presentation, key topical discussion or stop every 20 minutes to take questions.

- *Dedicate a time for Q&A.* Create a specific time to take questions from the audience, usually held at the end of the program and before the final summary.

How. Once you decide *when* you will take questions, determine *how* you are going to entertain questions from the audience.

Live. Take questions from the floor. There are three ways to get audience questions:

- *Queue.* Questioners line up at the microphone.
- *Runners.* With a cordless microphone, the support staff runs to questioners who have their hands raised in anticipation.
- *Oprah-Style.* The moderator roams the audience with a cordless microphone to take questions.

Screened. Filter and prioritize the questions, albeit with only short notice! There are four ways to screen their questions:

1. *Question Cards.* You can choose to pass out preprinted

question or note cards to the audience or have one placed on each chair as they enter the room. At a specific time in the session, the support staff circulates through the audience and collects the questions. You or one of your staff quickly sorts through the cards, selecting those that encapsulate key themes or ask an intriguing question. You can also have an audience member or panelist pull out a question card at random.

2. *Text or Tweet.* Invite the audience to text or tweet (or some other social media platform) with the appropriate hash tag or cell phone number. Watch the feed while the panel is going on, check the feed periodically, or ask staff to watch the feed for you

3. *Small Groups.* Break into small groups of three or four to discuss what questions they would like to ask. Pick random tables to ask their best question.

4. *Seeded.* Ask trusted audience members to ask a straightforward or supplied question at the beginning of the session or during a lull in the conversation.

Crowdsourced. Use a meeting app to enable the audience to create and "like" the questions so you simply pull the favorites from the top of the list!

Ground Rules. Think about the ground rules you want to put in place with the audience:

- *Stand.* Ask them to stand or move to a microphone so others can see the questioner.

- *State your Name and Organization.*

- *Panelist Name(s).* Who should answer the question.

- *One Sentence.* State the question in one sentence plus a few sentences to clarify, if needed.

Tips on Using SMS/Text Messaging & Twitter

- Ask a colleague or support person to be the "ombudsman" to monitor the "back channel" of tweets or text messages. Allow her to interrupt if there are any issues or questions that need to be addressed.
- Midpoint during the session, check in with the ombudsman and ask, "What's the buzz?" or "What are people liking or not liking?" Ask for issues that need clarification.
- If you can't find an ombudsman, you can periodically monitor the tweets or text messages through your phone or laptop. This can be hard to do while listening intently to the discussion, so take a "Twitter Break" every 10-15 minutes to check the back channel.

- Be prepared to shift the course of the discussion and adapt based on what you see in the back channel.
- Ask a few Twitterers to step forward to share their tweets (both positive and negative) with the entire audience.
- If you are brave, you can display the backchannel on a screen that everyone (including you) can see. While this can be visibly distracting for some, and others will submit asinine tweets (Hi Dad!), you can respond immediately to any issues that come up. As a precaution, explain how you will respond to the Twitter stream at the beginning of your presentation, and they will be more likely to use it responsibly.

Determine Logistics

The setup of the room is crucial to the success of the panel and shapes the way you can command the attention of the panelists and the audience. As a general rule, the cozier the better as you want to inspire a great conversation that everyone wants to hear.

Platform. In audiences of more than a hundred people, the panelists should be on a platform that allows everyone to see them – or have the panelists sit on high bar stool chairs that have a back and don't swivel.

Moderator Station. There is no "right" place to be located; just be aware of the pro's and con's of each:

- *Standing at a Lectern.* Although you have a place to put your notes, the lectern is a barrier between you and everyone else.

- *Stand On the Side.* The moderator stands stage right and is free to move about the stage. It may be harder to get eye contact and intervene with the panelists.

- *Seated Among the Panelists.* The moderator sits (rather than stands) stage right. It can be difficult to intervene.

- *Seated Between the Panelists.* Perfect for a debate format, this style enables you to intervene easily in either direction. It also makes you the focal point for the audience, splits the panel in half and makes it harder for the panelists to interact with each other.

- *In the Audience.* Often referred to as Oprah-style, this style makes you the center of attention. It is best when there are significant audience questions and interaction.

Furniture. The placement and type of furniture contributes to the ambiance. There are pro's and con's to each setup:

- *Formal.* Most panels are seated behind skirted tables where panelists can make notes and keep materials handy. Unfortunately, the table is a physical barrier that separates the panelists from the audience. It also diminishes the panelists' natural body language.

- *Informal.* Seat the panelists in a shallow semi-circle in comfortable chairs with a small cocktail table in front or to the side. Although their notes will be held in their laps, this eliminates the "barrier" between the panel and the audience, thus increasing the intimacy of the dialogue. (Note: If you do this, please let the panelists know. You'll be amazed to discover short skirts, holey (or no) socks and other wardrobe malfunctions!)

Water & Writing. Have water on the table plus paper pads and pencils available to allow the panelists to take notes.

Screen. Place the screen to the left of the stage (upstage right) and NOT behind the panel!

Bonus: Logistics Checklist

Think through all the logistics involved with your panel session. Coordinate with the meeting chair planner to make sure everything is ready to go!

www.PowerfulPanels.com

Microphones. For audiences under 50 people, you may be able to get away without using microphones. Between 50-75, it's nice to have. Over 75, use some kind of amplification system. Even if you don't think you need it, other people will appreciate it!

- *Panelists.* Each panelist should have an individual lavaliere microphone; however, budget or logistics may make it necessary to share. When sharing a microphone, a wireless handheld is preferable. If sitting at a table, a table microphone is acceptable.

- *Moderator.* The moderator should always have a lavaliere microphone or use the lectern microphone. When moving into the audience for Q&A, the moderator needs an additional wireless handheld to capture audience comments.

- *Audience.* If the moderator stays on the stage, you'll need to have a "runner" (or two) with a wireless microphone in hand OR a wireless or corded microphone on a stand in strategic places throughout the audience.

Recording Device. Even though the event might be professionally recorded, you may want to record the session yourself using your smart phone or other recording device.

Attire. Dressing professionally and appropriately helps establish your credibility and trustworthiness. Wear clean and pressed well-fitting clothes that either match or are slightly classier than what the audience is wearing. Wear a primary color that is NOT the same as or clashes with the backdrop. And don't forget to polish your shoes!

Confirm Details with the Panelists

Never assume that your panelists have done a panel before, so provide them with as much detail as you can to make sure they are clear about the expectations and comfortable with their role.

Pre-Event Email. Send them a pre-event email with the following information:

• *Panel Info.* Panel title, date, time, location, description, objectives and promotional material.

• *Panelist Info.* Names, short bios and websites of other panelists, where to register and where to meet up just prior to the start.

• *Panel Format.* How you plan to run the panel and the first one or two questions you intend to ask.

• *Audience.* Audience demographics and estimated size so panelists can bring the appropriate number of handouts, books, etc.

• *Room Setup.* Backdrop, chairs and platform configuration.

• *Presentations.* Specific instructions, e.g., time frames, slideshow format, getting the slideshows to you, etc.

• *A/V.* Audio-visual capabilities and requirements, e.g., microphones, coordination of video, presentation, etc.

• *Promotion.* Degree of appropriate self-promotion as well as use of social media.

• *Pre-Event Meet Up.* Ask if they are willing to join a brief call to plan the session and if so, best times times to call.

Pre-Event Meet Up. A short conference call or video conference (30 minutes) a week or two before the panel allows the opportunity for everyone to connect and hear the same information sent in the email as well as ask any format questions. **You don't want to conduct the panel beforehand, so keep this light and social.** If you believe there might be a lack of controversy or potential overlap in answers or opinions, you *may* want to probe each panelist's approach to the topic. It is also a nice touch to invite the meeting chair/planner to attend/listen in. Here are some key items to cover:

• *Welcome.* Set the tone for how excited you are.

• *Panel Info.* Panel title and objectives.

• *Self Introductions.* Name and two sentence focus area of expertise, approach or opinion. Be firm in enforcing the two sentence rule – you are modeling being an effective facilitator!

• *Audience.* Review the audience demographics and size.

• *Panel Format.* Review the format/agenda.

• *Questions.* Share the first few questions you will ask during the panel and see if there are any questions they want you to ask.

• *Props.* Encourage props or items to help the conversation or illustrate a key point.

• *Other?* Open the floor for any questions from the panelists.

• *Event Meet Up.* Confirm the time and location (speaker lounge, green room, etc.) to meet about an hour before the event to go over last minute issues.

Final Confirmation. Take notes during the pre-event meet up and email them to all panelists. This also serves as an excellent final confirmation of their participation.

Break Bread. Invite the panel to go to breakfast, lunch or dinner together, especially if they have not met. This is meant to be an opportunity to relax, get to know each other and build a rapport that will be obvious on stage. **It is NOT the place to hold the panel discussion!**

Bonus: Panelist Do's & Don'ts Tip Sheet

You can customize this tip sheet on Panelist Do's and Don'ts for your own use.

Include the tip sheet in with your emails to the participants.

www.PowerfulPanels.com

Assemble the Slideshow

In most cases, panels should focus on the discussion and interaction between panelists. Slides and slideshow presentations should be used only in the following situations:

- Adds value from the attendee's perspective

- Makes an abstract concept more visibly understandable

- Grabs the audience's attention

Otherwise, leave the slideshow for a different presentation format.

Bonus: Panelist PPT Template

You can customize this PowerPoint® slide template (see page 14) to introduce your panelists.

www.PowerfulPanels.com

Slide Ideas. Here are some ideas:

- *Panelist Slide.* One slide for each panelist with a photograph, name, a few key bullets and twitter handle. Display this slide when the panelist is introduced. Create a continuous loop of all the panelist slides to show as people are walking into the room, prior to the start of the session.

- *Panelist Summary Slide.* One slide with each panelist lined up in the same seating order with photo, headline and twitter handle. This stays up for the duration of the session. *(See example on page 14).*

- *Transition.* A funny, applicable video transition as the panel is getting set up or right after it is over.

- *Reference.* Allow each panelist to submit one (or other specific number) slide that they may need to reference during the conversation. If you allow more, then you need to allow ALL the panelists the same number of slides.

- *Set a Max.* As a general rule of thumb, a 60 minute panel can get through 15-20 slides and a panelist should speak to only 2-3 slides before giving the floor to another panelist. Set a max number of slides and amount of time.

Presentations. If you are going to allow panelists to present using visuals, encourage them to:

- Keep them brief and specific to the topic. Consider having additional information in a handout, takeaway or on a website rather than in the slides.

- Use the organization's defined format or template, if required.

- Include the panelist's contact name and information on their first slide.

- Keep the slideshow from being dependent on Wi-Fi. Although it may be accessible, it still may not work!

- Use video judiciously. It can gobble up precious time quickly.

Moderator Review. If possible, collect the presentations early to review the slides prior to the event to ensure panelists are addressing the topic, limiting their slide count and minimizing duplication among the panelists' presentations. Don't worry about making all the slides look the same – unless the organization has mandated it.

Combine. Assemble one overall slideshow file and stay in control of advancing the slide deck. Preload on a single computer so you eliminate the technical difficulties in making multiple laptops work with a single projector. Then, as your panelists speak, you (or the A/V tech) can easily bring up and advance their slides.

Last Minute Ideas. Beware of the clever panelist who wants to show a slide or video at the very last minute. Your answer should be a firm and pleasant, "No."

Spread the Word

No one really thinks about the moderator during the marketing and promotion process. Although you are not responsible for marketing the program, you can certainly help the meeting organizers promote the event and the panel session.

Alignment. Make sure the marketing materials and promotional promises match your agenda.

Upgrade. Take a look at the event app, promotional materials and website. At the very least, there should be a catchy title with a summary of what the audience will get out of it. Panelist and moderator bios are helpful along with their twitter usernames. If this information is not there, work with the meeting planners to get it in the program.

Social Media. Let everyone know about the upcoming wildly interesting panel discussion through social media channels. Your blog, Twitter, LinkedIn and Facebook are all great ways to promote your panel ahead of time and to solicit questions from the audience.

Survey. Create a short web-based survey for the attendees to complete prior to attending the event. Solicit questions and other details that would make the panel discussion truly engaging for them.

Twitter. Set up a twitter hash tag to solicit questions ahead of time and from the audience during the event. (Beware if you have two sessions going on at the same time with fervent twitterers. You might see some conflicting threads in the twitter stream.)

Video. Create a video teaser that explains the objective of the panel and the caliber of the panelists.

Invite Others. Send the promotional materials link to clients, potential customers and those you know who might be interested in attending the panel and/or event. Encourage your panelists to do likewise. After you moderate the panel, reach out to them again to let them know how it went. Share the key points discussed.

Self-Promotion. Beware of flagrant self-promotion. Make it about the event, the session and the audience, and not about you.

Example Panelist Summary Slide

Panel Title

Kristin Arnold	**Full Name**	**Full Name**	**Full Name**
Panel Moderator	Accolade	Accolade	Accolade
Professional Facilitator	Accolade	Accolade	Accolade
Award-Winning Author	Accolade	Accolade	Accolade
@kristinjarnold	@Twitter	@Twitter	@Twitter

Just Before It Starts

It's show time! The big day is finally here and it's time to put all that planning into action.

Arrive Early. You just never know what will happen on the way to the event, so get there in plenty of time.

Say Hello. As soon as you get to the venue, seek out your panelists to say "hello." Help them get settled and answer any last minute questions they have. Chances are they don't need your help, but they will appreciate the effort.

Check In. Once you know that everyone is present and accounted for, send a text message to the event chair/planner to let them know all is well. You may also want to get some feedback on how the conference is going, what areas and topics have been discussed and what areas still need to be addressed.

Walk Through. Walk through with the meeting planner, audio-visual crew and/or hotel personnel to check the:

- *Room Setup.* Review the stage lighting and furniture layout. If the room is too big, encourage the audience to sit toward the front by taping off the back rows. Make sure the panelists have water.

- *Microphones.* Test every single microphone to make sure that the people in the back of the room can hear the panelists clearly.

- *Slideshow.* Make sure your "clicker" will advance the slides or have the laptop directly in front of you. Open up the file(s) and go over the graphics one last time with the A/V crew.

- *Program.* Confirm what is occurring immediately before and after the session and any last minute directions you need to give to the audience.

- *Lights.* Don't leave your audience in the dark. House lights should be half to two-thirds up to spotlight the panel and encourage note taking by the audience.

Meet-Up. 45-60 minutes before the panel is to start, meet each other face to face for about 15 minutes. If a panelist cannot attend, make other arrangements to get together onsite prior to the panel. Make sure they are relaxed and prepared to have some fun! At this quick meeting:

- Review the format and agenda. Be firm with the panelists about the amount of time allocated to their initial comments and other ground rules.

- Hand out the agenda on one side and on the other side, have the seating plan and top 5 ground rules.

- Review the seating order and make sure it is consistent with your prepared slide.

- Review your introduction with each panelist for accuracy and relevance. Make sure you know how to pronounce their personal and company names correctly.

- Tell them how and when you will intervene and how they should signal to you and to each other when they want to answer a question.

- Remind the panelists to turn off their cell phones.

- Encourage the panelists to mingle with the crowd before the panel starts...and to have fun!

Resist the urge to discuss what you are going to talk about during the actual session. You want to keep the conversation fresh and lively.

Murphy's Law: Be Prepared

According to Murphy, whatever can go wrong, will go wrong. Have in your back pocket:

- **Back-up Agendas.** Conferences often run late, so allow your organizers to get back on schedule with agendas that have been modified to be 10, 15 or 30 minutes shorter.

- **Back-up Panelist.** Panelists often don't show up on time – or at all. Recover easily by having a back-up panelist who is prepared to step in if needed. Or a have a back-up agenda that accounts for a session with one less panelist!

Open the Session

The first few minutes of the session are critical. Although people shouldn't judge a book by its cover, they do. The audience (and panelists) need to know that they are in good hands.

- **Be Confident.** You've done your homework. You have a solid process in place. You know the panelists. You'll do great!

- **Start Strong.** You practiced these first few minutes and you *know* you are setting the tone, pace and energy for a powerful panel discussion.

The opening consists of five parts:

1. Topic Introduction. Welcome the audience and lead into the topic with a short, interesting hook that grabs their attention. DO NOT repeat verbatim what is in the program. Give it a fresh spin that rephrases and focuses on the promise.

2. You and Your Role. Take just a few moments to state your name, your affiliation, your qualifications to moderate the panel and a short definition of your role as moderator. 30 seconds, TOPS.

3. Agenda and Process. Let the audience know what is going to be covered, general guidelines about the process, ground rules, timing, and when and where to direct questions.

4. Housekeeping. There may be some announcements that need to be made, depending on your unique circumstances:

- *Handout Availability.* "There should be a handout for each participant as you walked in the door" or "These slides will be posted on SlideShare.net or the organization's website tomorrow."

- *Recording Instructions.* "This presentation is being taped so if you are asking a question, please step forward to a microphone." Or "If you don't want to be videotaped for this panel discussion, I suggest you sit on the left side of the room – out of the view of the camera."

- *Breaks.* For long panel formats, make a break schedule.

- *Phones.* Remind the audience to silence their cell phones, tweet with a hashtag, take pictures, etc.

5. Panelist Introductions. Regardless of whether you are doing the introducing or they are introducing themselves, you set the process in place. Remember, the whole point of doing introductions is to connect the audience with the panelists – who they may or may not know.

Either have all the panelists seated or bring them up one at a time. Make sure the panelists are viewed as competent and valuable. After all have been introduced, leave a summary picture/bio slide up so that the participants can easily recall which expert is speaking.

Watch for Snags. While all of this is going on, you need to be the eyes and ears of the audience. Can they hear you? Can they hear each panelist as they begin to speak? If at anytime you have doubts, ask, "Can everyone hear?" Don't hesitate to ask your panelists to talk closer to the microphone, if necessary. Ideally, the A/V staff, support staff or microphone runners can make you aware of any malfunctions as well.

Get the Conversation Started

Once the introductions to the topic and the panelists are done, the actual discussion starts. This is the toughest part of the moderator's job, and this is where the moderator can make the greatest difference.

Ground Rules. Remind the panelists and inform the audience of the ground rules for this portion of the program.

Master Multi-Tasking

Facilitating the discussion is not easy; you must master the art of multi-tasking: You must be

- Deeply listening to the current discussion,

- Thinking about the overall planned discussion,

- Watching the time, noting how long the current discussion has gone on,

- Balancing the participation of the panelists,

- Deciding where to take the conversation next,

- Thinking about the key points to summarize AND

- Keeping the needs of the audience ALWAYS at the forefront!

Use Your Questions. Get the panelists to talk by using your well-prepared conversation starter questions. Make it sound like you just thought of them and make sure each question is directed to a specific panelist.

Hot Potato or Ping Pong. The first question will take the form of conversational ping pong or a game of hot potato and then the conversation will evolve into more of a discussion.

Break Eye Contact. Look at the panelist when asking a question, then turn to the audience to gauge their reaction and interest. If you look at the panelists after you've asked a question, the panelist will instinctively look back at you when responding. You really want the panelists to talk to among themselves and with the audience!

Watch for Cues. In your pre-meeting, you set up a way for panelists to catch your eye to let you and the other panelists know that they would like to respond. Your speakers should be able to tell you and each other with a glance that they want to address a question or follow up on someone else's comments.

Two is Enough. Don't go down the hot potato line for every question. By the time the fifth panelist is answering the same question four other panelists have answered, the contribution is probably pretty thin. When you ask a question, two answers is plenty, unless a third person is dying to jump in.

Be Flexible. Be open and flexible about following the natural conversation path as long as it is interesting and the audience is engaged. Be willing to let go of your planned questions should a particularly interesting line of discussion emerge.

Take Notes. Especially when the panelists deliver prepared remarks, listen very carefully and take notes. Wherever possible, capture important statements verbatim so you can refer to them during the discussion.

Invite Comments. Encourage other panelists to comment on particular parts of other panelists' statements. Stay away from a general, "What do you think about that?" It opens the door to off topic answers.

Use Humor. Use humor gently and appropriately in service of the discussion. Use your natural wit to lighten the moment. Beware of going too far with canned jokes, gimmicks and sarcasm. It's a panel, not a game show.

Banter. Encourage the panelists to have fun, chatter and joke among themselves.

Keep the Conversation Moving at a Brisk Pace

If you have prepared the panelists appropriately and kicked it off well, the conversation will start to flow on its own and the panelists won't be coming back to you for ping-pongs or hot potatoes. However, you may need to interject here and there to keep the conversation moving at a brisk pace. An energy lull can be devastating.

Ask Follow-Up Questions. Build on what has been said to deepen or extend the thinking. "You mentioned X. Could you tell us more about that? How did you accomplish so much in such little time?"

5Ws & 1H: Aim for application to the real world versus a lot of theory. Explore the issues with impromptu and relevant questions that start with Who, What, Where, When, Why and How.

Probe Deeper. When a panelist makes a claim that just doesn't sound quite right, question it on behalf of the audience. Ask for an example, metrics or sources to substantiate the claim.

Make Bridges. Look for opportunities to connect two ideas together. "Andy, that's an interesting point you just made about A. Cathy, earlier you referenced B. Are these two ideas related? Do you need one to accomplish the other?"

Connect the Dots. Listen carefully to the comments and then pose a question that infers a logical consequence of the previous comments. "Betsey, you mentioned X and Y. I was wondering if Z holds true?"

Stir the Pot. Look for areas of disagreement between panelists. Ask a panelist for a contradictory point of view. "Brian just stated X. Alice, what is your view on X?"

Ask for the Devil. If the panel is in complete agreement, don't just stir the pot because you can. Although, if you know that there is something deeper to explore, ask a panelist or an audience member to serve as a "devil's advocate" and argue the other side of the issue.

Catch Contradictions. You have to be on your toes to catch panelists contradicting themselves. "Charlie, you just mentioned X, and earlier you mentioned Y. That seems at odds with each other. Please clarify your position."

Test the Unsaid. If you sense there is something which hasn't been said, test the waters to bring out the unspoken issue. "We seem to be skirting around the issue. Could it be Z?"

Shift Gears. When you have covered one topic enough, don't be afraid to shift the focus of the conversation to another topic.

Create Transitions. Before you move on from one topic to another, summarize the key points and bring it back to the core topic. These transitions should mark key threads in the conversation.

Be Neutral. Never say "I agree with..." Your role is to be neutral and facilitate the conversation, not to weigh in and offer your opinion.

Be Quiet. You don't need to interject a question, comment or make a witty observation after each panelist speaks. Let the conversation flow...until it isn't flowing as well.

Heads Up. Two minutes before the end of this section, let the audience know that you will be moving into the next section (usually audience Q&A), the process you will be using (line up at the microphone, raise hands, use SMS, tweet) and the ground rules. This gives them time to think about their questions so you can launch right into the Q&A session.

Bonus: Tips to Engage the Audience

You can engage the audience throughout the panel discussion – not just during Q&A.

Check out these quick tips at www.PowerfulPanels.com

Intervene Firmly and Respectfully

As the moderator, you are the audience's chief advocate. If someone's boring you, then chances are they are boring the audience as well. If you think they are going on too long and not making their point, you need to intervene.

The good news about your panel of experts is that they know A LOT about their issue and are used to talking extensively about it. You need to make sure they understand the ground rules and when and how you will intervene.

Prevention Strategies. The best way to intervene is to prevent the problem from happening in the first place. Then, when they do "step over the line" you can point to one of the prevention strategies or ground rules you have put into place:

• Reinforce the topic/purpose etc. at the beginning.

• Alert speakers to the fact that all time limits will be strictly observed.

• Create a signal for them as they come to the end of their time limit.

Escalating Interventions. Be firm, polite and fair. Start with the lowest level intervention appropriate to the situation. If that doesn't modify the disruptive behavior, then kick it up a notch to the next level intervention.

Do Nothing. You always have the option to do nothing and see if the situation resolves itself. However, if you let one person run over, you penalize everyone else.

Eye Contact.

• Shoot 'em a glance when their time is almost up or they are making inappropriate or irrelevant comments.

• Confidently check your watch.

Movement.

• Move toward them, show a cue card. tap your pencil, or ring a bell.

Redirect the Conversation.

• Change up the questions.

• Restate or reframe the question and direct it to another panelist.

• Rephrase the statement into something more relevant.

• Condense a panelist's answer when it is too lengthy.

• Call on someone in the audience who you know has similar issues and ask if what was just said vibes with them.

• Gently interrupt and assure them that you can return to discussing X later in the panel if there is enough time.

• Interject at the end of a sentence or while the panelist is taking a breath.

• Ask for one conversation at a time when panelists are talking over each other.

• Transition to the next topic when the topic has been covered enough.

Remind Them.

• Refocus on the topic.

• Reinforce the process ground rules.

• Restate the time allocated for the comment.

• Reinforce a key point.

• Announce the time remaining for this section of the panel.

Confront the Disrupter. This is the highest level intervention and you should only have to resort to this level if you have a jerk on your panel.

• Appeal to the disrupter.

• Cut off the speaker.

• Disengage.

The moderator is called the moderator because her role is to ensure that there is only a moderate level of bull shitake and sales pitches. A good moderator is the audience's advocate for truth, insight, and brevity—any two will do. When a panelist makes a sales pitch or tells lies, you are morally obligated to smack him around in front of the audience.

Guy Kawasaki
Advisor to Motorola
Former chief evangelist of Apple

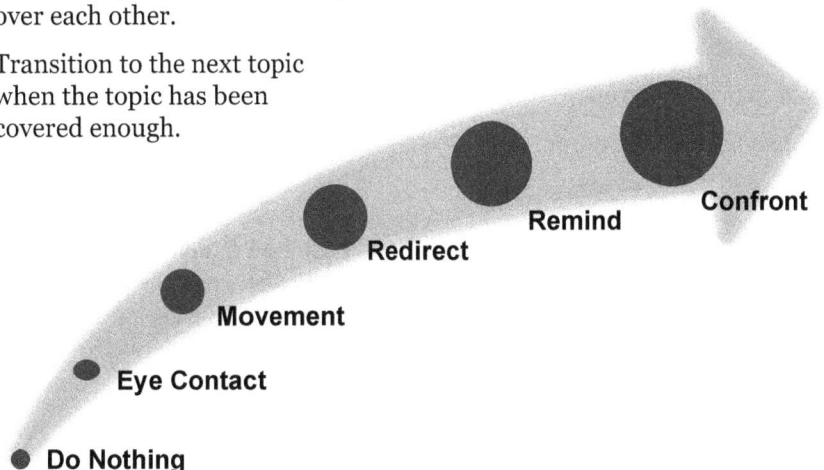

Confront

Remind

Redirect

Movement

Eye Contact

Do Nothing

Facilitate the Audience Q&A

At some point during the session, the moderator will ask for questions from the audience via text, question card, open microphone or Oprah-style, depending on the event.

Describe the Process. Share the process you will use to solicit questions *(see page 10)*. Then follow the process. Don't deviate for anybody.

Review the Ground Rules. For example, "Please stand, state your name and organization, the name of the panelist you are directing the question to, your one sentence question and a few sentences to clarify your question if necessary… and panelists, please speak to the audience when answering all the questions. Now, what questions do you have?"

Repeat the Question. Repeat, restate or summarize the question for the entire audience to hear and for it to get on any recordings being made. Reframe tangential questions to be more on topic.

Prompt a Panelist. When the question is for anyone on the panel, restate the question and then direct the question to a panelist who:

- Is signaling to you
- You feel would best answer it
- Has not responded as much

Hot Potato the Question. If a panelist is not being asked questions by the audience, you can say, "John, that was a great answer. Mary, do you feel the same way?"

Queue. If a large number of people raise their hands at the start of the Q&A session, start with the first person who raised a hand and establish a "queue" or lineup that lets the audience know who will go next.

- *Follow the Queue.* Once you establish the order, doggedly follow it. If you have a hard time remembering the order, write it down or enlist someone to help you keep track.

- *Add to the Queue.* While a panelist is answering a question, you may see someone new raising their hand. You can point to the person and nod, signaling that the person will be next in the queue.

- *Call on the Questioner.* Call on them by name if you know them or can read their nametags. Otherwise, use some defining, flattering feature: "The lovely lady in the bright red jacket, please give us your question in one sentence."

Work the Room. Make sure that the questions are spread among different members within the audience. Try to hear from everyone who has a question before you return to someone for a second turn. You can even offer that you are looking for new faces to chime in before you let a repeat questioner back in the queue.

Prevent Speeches. You and your microphone runners should NEVER let go of the microphone.

Last Two Questions. Warn the audience when the session is drawing to a close and that you have time for one or two more questions.

What to Do When the Inbound Question is…

Unfocused or Unclear. Rephrase the question as close to the questioner's words and intention and check for agreement. Or, ask for the person to "headline" the question.

Weak. Rather than restating or merely repeating the question, tweak a weak question to make it better than it is. Check with the questioner to make sure that is what was meant.

Too Specific, Detailed or Complex. Suggest the questioner talk with the panelist immediately after the session. "That's an interesting question, and perhaps better addressed in depth by Panelist A after the wider Q&A we're doing now."

Long Winded. Firmly but politely remind the questioner to state the question. "What is your question?" "Get to the question, please" or "Is there a question in there?"

A Comment. Intervene quickly when the audience member says, "I don't have a question, it's more of a comment…." Quickly state, "The panelists will be available for comments at the end" and then move briskly to the next questioner.

Conclude the Session

Let the audience know that the program is coming to an end by saying, "We're almost out of time... Just a few key things to wrap up."

Summarize the Discussion.
Look at your notes and transition statements to summarize the discussion. There are several ways to do this, and make sure you include a sentence or two about each speaker's contribution:

- *Top Three Insights.* You've been taking notes, so share the top three insights that seemed to resonate with the audience.

- *Big Picture.* Share an integrated view of what has been said. Point out the convergences and divergences of viewpoints while remaining neutral yourself.

- *Personal View.* Link back to your opening and share what you heard, what you learned, and why it's important to the field.

- *One Final Thought.* Offer each panelist a last opportunity to share a key point, what the *panelist* is taking away from the conversation, or a future-forward question such as "What important new trend will we be talking about at next year's conference?"

Best Contact Info. Let the panelists share where they can be found online or where others can learn more about them. Model the final statement for them as, "I work at company U in V role. I can be found online at W."

Promotional Kicker. Allow the panelists to let the audience know something about them or their company e.g. when their upcoming product release will be.

Thank You. Quickly thank the audience, conference sponsors, meeting chair/planner, A/V crew and each panelist by name.

Gifts. If there are gifts for the panelists, have them ready to hand out or show the audience ONE of the gifts that you'll give each panelist after the session is over. Present the gift to each panelist right then and there or immediately after the panel.

Extend the Conversation. Invite the audience to extend the conversation in the front of the room, in the hallway or in the bookstore immediately after the end of the session. You can also encourage the discussion to move online to the conference website, blog, wiki, forum or social media platform group (e.g., Facebook, LinkedIn). Share any additional resources available to the attendees. Encourage any photographers to post their pictures.

Final Announcements. Encourage the audience to attend the next activity following the panel and alert the audience to upcoming events, future programs, handouts, evaluation forms, educational credit forms and other details as necessary.

Lead the Applause. Ask the audience to join you in expressing appreciation with their applause. Start clapping and the audience will clap, too!

Finish on Time. Do not go past your scheduled end time. The audience will get restless and start to leave.

Don't Rush Away. Stay in the room or designated spot to continue the conversation. Talk to anyone who comes up to you and stay until their questions have been answered.

The panel method...has all the delight of generous give-and-take. And if it is a genuinely good conversation, it sends people away with a warm feeling not only that their own ideas have been clarified but that their understanding of other points of view have been broadened.

Harry A. Overstreet
Originator of the Panel
as a Discussion Method (1934)

Congratulations! You have moderated an amazingly successful panel discussion. You met the panel objectives, delivered on the promise, made the panelists look like heroes and the audience received tremendous value.

But it's not over...yet.

Seek Out Others. For the remainder of the conference, seek out those people who were highly engaged and connect with them sometime during the conference. You'll build some great relationships!

Question Cards. Collect the question cards and coordinate responses from the panelists. Feed the answers into the organization's newsletter, Frequently Asked Questions (FAQs) or other communications vehicle.

Critique. Within 24 hours after the session, make a few notes about what you liked and what you might do differently for the next time you moderate a panel discussion.

Debrief. Chat with the meeting chair/planner about the session. Review the evaluation forms from the audience. Ask if there was anything they would have liked you to do differently so you can do a better job next time.

Thank You's. Send a personal note, card or email to each panelist, the meeting chair/coordinator and anyone else who made your life easier. Thank them for doing such a great job – and add something specific about what they did or said that contributed to the panel's success.

Summary Report. Using your notes and Twitter feed, provide a written summary of the panel discussion to the meeting chair that includes:

• Short description of the panel

• Panelist names

• Estimated audience size

• Brief summary of the discussion

• Conclusions

• Recommendations for future panels

Repurpose Your Summary. Take the tidbits of wisdom from your summary and:

• Post the highlights, key quotes and photos on the event website, social media, etc.

• Post the slides on Slideshare.net.

• Write a blog about your experience.

• Share the summary with key clients and potential customers.

Recordings. The meeting chair/planner may post the professional audio file, video file and/or transcript on the web for others to read or, with their permission, post your own recording. Provide links and take excerpts from the transcript to use in follow-up communications to panelists and post-conference communications.

Keep Learning. Review your own performance. Watch others. Attend other conferences and see how different people moderate. Learn what works for them and what doesn't. Integrate your learning into each subsequent panel you moderate or participate in!

Want More?

Yes, there is more. The body of knowledge about the panel format used at meetings, conferences and conventions continues to grow and it will never stop growing. It will continually get better as we add to the body of knowledge about facilitating panel discussions. We call it the "Powerful Panels Knowledge Vault."

You can purchase lifetime access to the Knowledge Vault - chock-full of best practices, customizable checklists, worksheets, templates, scripts, specialty format agendas, sample emails, PowerPoint® templates, video examples of the good, the bad and the ugly, video interviews with industry icons and professional moderators, recorded webinars and slideshows, industry reports on the effectiveness of panels...and more! It's a one-stop shop – one place to find out anything you need to know about moderating panels.

Find out more about joining the powerful panel community at www.PowerfulPanels.com

Read on for an excerpt from Kristin Arnold's award winning book, *Boring to Bravo*. Available in hardcover and ebook formats at online bookstores and www.ExtraordinaryTeam.com.

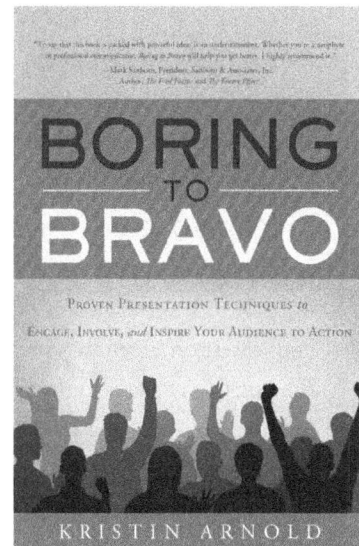

CHAPTER SIX

ASK ENGAGING QUESTIONS

A KEY SKILL for any presenter is to ask questions that stimulate the audience's thinking and get them involved. Questions enable you to continue the conversation, so set the tone for audience participation and collaboration by asking a few engaging questions early on in your presentation.

The key to asking engaging questions is to be thoughtful and deliberate. Keep in mind that you can turn off an audience with random, nonsensical queries.

When crafting an engaging question, be sure to consider the following points.

KNOW THY PURPOSE. Know why you are asking the question: to create discussion, to introduce controversy, to elicit a response or opinion, to review information, to provide insight, to determine their level of understanding, and so forth.

BE MEANINGFUL. Make sure your questions are meaningful to your audience, not just to you. Get rid of the truly stupid or patronizing questions that insult rather than inspire the audience (e.g., "Who here would like to be rich?" or "How many of you have children, or have ever been a child?"). When the answer is patently obvious, you have no business asking them such a trite question. Tee up something meaningful about your topic that will elicit diversity of thought in the room.

KEEP 'EM GUESSING. Your audience doesn't know whether you expect an answer from them until your presentation continues. You can ask the question and answer it, or you can address a question to an individual, or you can poll the larger group. Don't rely on one questioning technique.

HAVE TWO RIGHT ANSWERS. Don't put the audience in the awkward position of knowing that you have a "right" answer in mind. It just isn't fair—unless you are giving them a quiz. If your purpose is to advance the dialogue, craft your question carefully so there isn't a right or a wrong answer. Think through the possible answers so that you are comfortable with wherever the conversation needs to go.

SUFFER THE SILENCE. After you ask a question, pause a moment. Let the participants think. Then answer.

ADD VARIETY. Use various questioning styles and techniques in your presentation rather than boring your audience with just one or two techniques.

The rest of this chapter will focus on helping you add variety with various questioning techniques.

ASK AN OPEN-ENDED QUESTION ⚠️ ⚠️

Want to get the conversation started? Use an open-ended question—that is, one whose answer requires a sentence, not just a word or two. Open-ended questions usually start with the 5Ws and an H: Who, what, where, when, why, and how. A well-crafted open-ended question literally opens up the conversation space and encourages interaction with you.

Open-ended questions are like a tennis game. You serve one up and an answer comes back. Then you ask another, more specific question, and another, more specific answer comes back. As you volley back and forth with different participants, you'll move from general open-ended questions to more specific ones.

Make the question itself interesting. For example, you could ask, "What do you want to know?" or you could ask, "What is your one burning question you want answered today?" Which question do you think is more engaging?

Reserve the use of closed questions (i.e., those that have a yes/no or single word answer) to reinforce or punctuate a point in your presentation or to close the conversation and move on to the next point in your speech. (Just take a look at the paragraph immediately above for an effective use of an open-ended question followed by a closed question!) If you are going to use a closed question to introduce a point, set up the question so that you are ready to elaborate on it regardless of whether the answer is a "yes" or a "no."

Asking good questions is a skill to be acquired. Ask any teenager an open-ended question and they can clam up with a closed answer. Or ask any windbag a closed question and they can talk for hours. If you are not getting the response you are looking for, ask a different question. Keep the conversation flowing.

EXPERIMENT: ASK A GOOD QUESTION

Try *not* to think about this open-ended question: "What have you found most interesting in this book so far?" Didn't you find it difficult not to respond? Even if I don't like your answer, I have engaged you in a dialogue.

ASK A SITUATIONAL QUESTION ⚠

When you ask a situational question, you are asking the participants about their own experiences that are directly related to the content of your presentation. This type of question helps them recall or envision a time when they have been in a similar situation.

- Have you ever had . . . ?
- Did you ever find . . . ?
- How many times have you . . . ?
- When is the last time you . . . ?
- Do you sometimes . . . ?
- Have any of you tried to do [this]?
- Have you ever wondered . . . ?
- Remember how you felt when . . . ?
- Has [this] ever happened to you?
- Did you read/hear today about . . . ?
- Do you remember a time when you . . . ?
- If [this] happened, what would you do?

Situational questions are usually used to introduce the problem your presentation will solve or the goal to be achieved. Also, did you notice the word "you" is in every question? "You" is the focal point to a situational question because you are extending the situation beyond your experience into the audience's experience. It challenges the listeners to open up their file drawer of memories, flip through their current experiences so they can connect, and file the new information you will share with them.

ASK A PROVOCATIVE QUESTION ⚠ ⚠ ⚠

There is a momentous scene in the movie *Mona Lisa Smile* when Julia Roberts is teaching her first art history class at the conservative, Ivy League Wellesley Women's College in 1953. The house lights are off in a cavernous classroom when an enormous slide projector displays the first of what appears to be a progression of slides. The teacher asks, "Can anyone tell me what this is?" and one of the preppy girls promptly responds, "Wounded Bison, Altamira, Spain, about 15,000 BC." Another primitive drawing goes up and a different girl chimes in with the correct answer. The tempo of the answers increases, and we get the idea that the teacher doesn't have anything new to offer these students. We assume the teacher is devastated.

In the next sequence Roberts shows her students a curious painting they have never seen before. She lets them squirm and then asks a provocative question: "Is it any good?" Instead of spitting out a correct answer, her rote students have been challenged to *think* about what makes something art, and so the dialogue begins to flow.

When you ask a provocative question, you are encouraging the audience to think deeper about your topic. Some ways to create provocative questions include

- Take a key word from your presentation and ask the group to define it. ("We're talking about 'disruptive' technologies. What does 'disruptive' really mean to you?")

- Challenge the audience's assumptions. ("What do you know to be absolutely true about this topic?")

- Identify barriers. ("What will get in the way of our success?")

- Walk in another's shoes. ("How would your CEO answer that question?")

- Reflect the mood. ("What about this topic makes you angry?")

- Prioritize. ("What is the number one thing we should discuss today?")

- Provoke. ("What would it take for you to say yes to this proposal?")

The best provocative questions tap into the audience's knowledge of as well as their internal beliefs about your topic. So the risk is not so much in asking the question as it is in dealing with each participant's response.

HOW TO USE QUESTIONS TO DRIVE THE AGENDA

Having the audience drive the agenda is not for the faint of heart. You must truly have an engaging mind-set (see chapter 1) and the courage to go with the flow, to stray from your "script" and brave the rapids. Of course, you can quell your fears by thinking through the possible answers and figuring out how you can weave participants' answers into your presentation.

1. Ask an intriguing or provocative question, such as, "What is the biggest challenge you are facing in your business today?" You can respond to the first answer and that becomes your point number one. Reach out and ask for another answer to your question and that response becomes point number two, and so forth.

2. Make a list. You can simply listen to the ideas the group generates and make a mental list, or you can write their ideas on an easel chart or type them into the computer if you are really talented. When you write the ideas down, you can step back, look at the list, and circle the most pervasive items. Tell the audience your list and start with the most obvious and work your way through your list.

3. Summarize. You can take the top three themes that emerge and start with the first theme as your first point, the second theme as your second point, and so on.

ASK A RHETORICAL QUESTION ⚠

When you ask a rhetorical question, you do not expect a direct response from the audience; however, you do expect them to answer it in their heads. Many speakers (and audiences) confuse a rhetorical question with the technique of taking a poll, in which you expect them to give you a response to your closed question.

Phrase your rhetorical question for maximum impact by emphasizing key words you want the group to consider. After you pose the question, suffer a few seconds of silence. Patiently and calmly give all attendees enough time to collect their thoughts and answer the question in their own minds. Then, answer the question.

This technique is a favorite among many speakers; however, you can spoil the effect by asking the obvious question or rushing in to answer your own question too quickly, without giving your audience a chance to think about their own answers. Even worse, you could ask a barrage of meaningless rhetorical questions—one right after another—with the result that participants will simply disengage from the monotony.

TAKE A POLL ⚠ ⚠

When you take a poll or an on-the-spot quick survey or quiz, you are expecting the audience to respond to your question en masse.

It makes sense to take a poll if you really want to know the information *and* if you are in a room where you can see the participants. (Sometimes the house lights are turned down so low you may not be able to see the results of your poll, so this technique won't work well.)

When presenting to off-site locations, think through how you are going to get their feedback, either through using the conferencing technology or by calling them out. I like to create a sign or picture of the remote locations or specific participants, just so I can remember to call on them!

Especially during technical presentations to left-brained engineers, lawyers, and physicians, take a poll periodically throughout your presentation to stimulate discussion and showcase the diversity of thought within the audience.

You can poll the audience through a number of ways:

- Round-robin. Go around the room and ask each person to state his or her position.

- Show of hands. Ask those who agree with your question to raise their hands.

- Thumbs. Have those who agree with the point you just made show you a thumbs-up and those who don't a thumbs-down. A sideways thumb can mean "undecided."

- Stand up. Ask those in agreement or who find the statement to be true to stand up. Those who find your statement to be false can remain seated.

- Noise. Clap to agree and stomp to disagree. Or, if confidentiality is important, ask those who agree to hum. You'll find those who are passionate will hum loudly!

- Shout. Say "Of course!" if you agree and "No way!" if you don't. The volume can also show the strength of the person's commitment.

- Response cards. Ask participants to select and hold up the appropriate color-coded card/paper that signifies their response. These are ideal for multiple-choice and true-false questions or those with a range of responses (agree/neutral/disagree; high/medium/low). (See the caution about color in chapter 5.) 🔎

- Continuum. Have one side of the room take one stance (definitely) and the other side the polar opposite (no way!), or think of your own clever scale ("vested" to "don't care").

HOW TO TAKE A POLL

♦ Ask the question and model the behavior you want. For example, "Who here . . ." and while you are asking the question, raise your hand high in the air. This sends a clear signal that you are expecting those people who can say yes will raise their hand with you.

♦ Suffer the silence while people decide and move.

♦ Report the result. You are the one person in the room who can see all the results, and inquiring minds want to know. Share the results in the form of a statistic: "That looks like thirty folks, so that's 10 percent of the group." (Want to make it a tad bit funny? Report out the numbers in a precise way, even though it is obviously a best guesstimate. For example, you could say, "27 folks agree, and that is 13.3 percent of the group."

♦ You can also zoom in on a couple of people near you and ask them some more questions.

Hint: Do a dry run, especially if you are using response cards or an electronic polling technique.

USING TECHNOLOGY ⚠️ ⚠️ ⚠️ ⚠️

I was listening to a presentation to seventy-five people not so long ago when a cell phone went off. Everyone took their attention from the speaker to glance at their phone perched on their belt or buried in their purse. It is downright embarrassing for everybody. It will happen to you sometime, so keep a few throwaway lines to lighten the tension:

- If it's for me, tell them I'm busy.

- Go ahead, answer it; we'll wait.

- That's probably my mother calling to see if I met a nice girl/boy in Philadelphia.

- Domino's Pizza. You'd like a pepperoni and mushroom pizza?

Ever since the humble cell phone wiggled its way into the meeting room speakers have been admonishing their audiences to turn off their cell phones. However, you can encourage the opposite and embrace the use of cell phones and laptops. Ninety-nine percent of your audience members already have a cell phone in hand, so why not use it to inspire audience interaction? There are some evolving technologies where you can pose a question to the audience and they can reply via SMS text messaging on a cell phone or their laptops.

You can also ask everyone to tweet. Just let them know where to aim their comments (your cell phone, Twitter, or some other online medium), and let it go. Admittedly, it is tough to look out into an audience and see a few people with their heads down, looking at their devices. Get over it. Assume they are taking copious notes or twittering great things about your presentation. Another side benefit is that the conversation is then magnified *outside* of the venue as other people can tap into it!

Dial it up another notch and you can use an audience response system (ARS). Such a system is typically built into your PowerPoint presentation, allowing the audience to select or dial in an option from a remote keypad. The software automatically tabulates the results and displays it in a chart, table, or other format for the presenter and the audience to view. If you choose to use an ARS, you will need to plan the questions (or at least most of them) in advance, and you will need to be extremely comfortable with the technology to make the experience seamless with your presentation.

ASK A SERIES OF "ENROLLING" QUESTIONS

Close to the beginning of your presentation, you may want to ask a series of "enrolling" questions that tap into the audience's expectations or fears. It can also give you a focus in case you were not able to do an appropriate amount of exploration prior to the presentation.

When taking an informational survey, use the same techniques as for a poll, using the following preface: "Let's see by a show of hands/cards how all of you would answer the following questions." For example, if you wanted to explore their base of knowledge, you could phrase your questions this way:

- How many of you have heard of this topic?
- How many of you have some expertise in this area?
- How many of you think you should be up here giving this presentation?

Make your first question as inclusive as possible without being too basic or insulting, and limit yourself to three questions. No more. More than three, the audience will tire of raising their hand, stomping their feet, or waving a card at you. You can use the humorist's "Rule of Three" and make the last question a bit funny (see chapter 8).

ENCOURAGE ANSWERS FROM THE AUDIENCE

To continue the conversation with your audience you'll need them to respond to your questions. Encourage them to respond in several ways:

- They can just think about your question or comment. No verbal response is necessary with a rhetorical question.
- They can shout out an answer or freewheel.
- They can each answer in turn around the room.

- They can raise their hands and you select someone to answer.
- They can write it down on their handout or notepad for personal use.
- They can write it down on preprinted index cards or sticky notes.
- They can share their answer with a neighbor (dyad) or in groups of three (triad).

After you ask a great question, suffer the silence. Let the audience fill the space. Patiently and calmly give the audience time to collect their thoughts and the courage to raise their hands, shout out the answer, or write it down. Look as though you expect an answer, because you do. If you force yourself not to provide the answer, you will find that someone will *always* respond. Your audience will find the silence much more disturbing than you do.

Still nervous? By using a movement such as cupping your ear or putting both palms out, invite the group to shout out their answers You can even prod your audience by saying "Tell me!" Select and acknowledge a response in order to build a connection not only with the responder but also with the entire audience.

PARAPHRASE ANSWERS. Paraphrase or clarify someone's answer, especially if the entire room is not able to hear it. Create a headline; build on the answer and empathize with it.

ANCHOR HEADLINES. You may choose to validate several answers by writing them down on an easel chart. This anchors the comments and lets you return to them if necessary.

MAKE IT UNIVERSAL. Check with the rest of the room to understand and empathize with the responder. Ask, "Does anyone else have an experience similar to this?"

OPEN UP THE DIALOGUE. Challenge the group to add to the ideas and bring a fresh perspective by asking, "What do the rest of you think about what was said?" You can even be the contrarian to make the dialogue more lively.

ASK FOR EXAMPLES. Extend the response by asking for examples, explanations, or other opinions. Turn the Q&A into an experience that the entire room can share.

You can go the extra mile and create value that extends past your presentation by taking the results from the question (the easiest way to capture this information is from the easel chart or the index cards) and collate the data. Synthesize the results and send a copy to the meeting sponsor, meeting planner, and/or the participants. You can also write an article for the company newsletter, draft a "white paper" using the results, and even post the results on the company's or your own website.

INTERVIEW A PARTICIPANT
⚠ ⚠ ⚠ ⚠

You are probably wondering, "Why would I want to interview anybody as part of my program?" Good question. A simple interview helps you connect with a single person in the audience. And because your audience knows that this part of your program cannot be totally rehearsed, you create a deeper sense of connection with everyone in the room—particularly if your interview is interesting.

Take Oprah, for instance. She has spent her entire career interviewing others, but we all feel connected to her as an individual. By watching her quiz, answer, ask, and respond to so many people, we not only learn about her guests, we grow closer and more connected to her too.

When you invite an audience member to be in the limelight with you, you are placing him in a highly vulnerable position. The person doesn't know what to expect—and neither does the audience! It is reality TV up close and personal. Unfortunately, your volunteer is not going to win a million dollars for participating, so it is imperative that you create a risk-free, comfortable climate for him. You never want to embarrass your audience volunteer and never pressure or coerce someone into participating. If, based on what you know of the group, you think you'll have to pressure someone to participate, either start with someone you have chosen and coached before your presentation or reconsider using this technique.

When interviewing an audience member, consider the following steps, which depend on your personality and style, your tolerance for risk, and your audience's history. If they aren't used to being called upon, you may need to increase their comfort zone before they can participate.

SELECT. Consider asking for a volunteer who is excited and energized to talk with you *or* preselecting a participant based on your prework. Be cautious in calling on people randomly, as that conjures up memories of being singled out at school when you weren't prepared.

MEET THEM. Go out into the audience to meet with them *or* ask them to come up front with you.

REASSURE THEM. Tell them that it's going to be okay, how great they are for volunteering, and that you are not going to make them look silly or do something stupid. Whisper reassurances in their ear or use positive body language that puts them at ease. You can even involve the audience by saying: "Isn't Sally doing great? It's so awesome that she has volunteered!" Be warned, however; if a person telegraphs her displeasure at being volunteered by someone else, ask a simple question and let her off the hook quickly.

ASK THE QUESTION. Ask an open-ended question that creates a connection or rapport with the person. Use his name first, and then ask the question. If you are using a microphone (preferably a cordless handheld one), don't let him grab it because he may take it as an invitation to talk a while longer.

BE IN THE MOMENT. Roll with the answers. Give the group positive feedback. Have fun, because if you're having fun they will too. After two or three more questions and some banter back and forth, ask a closed question to end the conversation.

THANK 'EM. Don't forget to thank each of your volunteers for participating and let them go back to their seat! Always be doing something with your interviewee; do *not* keep anyone standing on stage with nothing to do.

HOW TO INTERVIEW A PARTICIPANT WITH A TOUCH OF HUMOR
Brad Montgomery, CSP

Our audiences are craving an experience, not a speech. They don't want somebody to deliver a "one-man show" or monologue. They want a presenter who makes the speech feel like a dialogue. The interview technique lets the audience connect with you as a presenter and experience the session in a way that is interactive, fresh, and rewarding to them. And because they know that these parts of your presentation cannot be totally rehearsed, the connection we form with them is deeper. And the results can be funny. Sometimes hilariously funny. Got it? Connection first, funny second.

So how do we do it? Simple: ask good open-ended questions that cannot be answered with one word. You could ask, "What would you be doing if you weren't here?" Sometimes they will answer with something boring like, "Well, I'd just be on shift, making sales calls." That's not funny, but that's okay because at least you have interacted with the audience and are a tiny bit more connected. On the other hand, you might get an awesome answer such as, "I'd be home watching reruns of *Hogan's Heroes* and eating a bag of fried pork skins." Trust me, crazy and funny answers like this one happen more than you might guess, and the result is fantastic. This sort of answer would stop the program with laughter, and you didn't do a darned thing but ask an engaging question.

Another good one: "What is your secret passion?" You'll find that just by asking this question you'll often get a chuckle, partly because there is an element of innuendo to the query, and the answers you get will be priceless. You might get an honest answer, such as "I'm really into remote-controlled airplanes." In this case, you'd just follow up with: "No kidding, remote-controlled air-planes? That sounds so great. Well, I'm so glad you're here." Cool—you're a bit closer to your audience!

Or you might get something like, "Well, nothing I can tell you about," which will earn a laugh. If you're lucky, it'll get a huge laugh. Sometimes people will answer this "Have any passions?" question with just a simple no. That answer is a disaster, right? No! It's funny! Note that all three types of answer—serious, offbeat, or dead end—are great for you. You get a chance to con-nect—and maybe even get a laugh.

If you ask good questions, you will improve your program regardless of the answers.

WRONG ANSWERS AND OTHER MALADIES ⚠ ⚠ ⚠

Sometimes the answer is just plain wrong or completely off base. You need to be able to handle these "wrong" answers just as gracefully as you do a correct answer.

ACKNOWLEDGE THE EFFORT. Acknowledge incorrect answers with a positive response, such as "That's interesting. Let's come back to that in a minute" or "Thanks for sharing your perspective, Sally."

ADD TO. Add to the question with a subtle redirection by saying, "Let me add to that . . ." or "There's another factor to consider when you are looking at . . ."

REFRAME. Reframe the question and disperse the question to include others. "Let's take a look at this from a different perspective . . ."

RECAP. When recapping the discussion, you can summarize the fact that there are a lot of opinions about the subject. Then explain the correct answer in detail.

ARGUMENTATIVE PEOPLE

Argumentative people aren't looking for an answer. They are looking for recognition. When you have an argumentative person in your audience, stay calm, cool, and collected. Recognize their expertise, but don't let them take over your presentation!

- Allow them to say their piece.
- Paraphrase their issue, reflecting the meaning and voicing the feeling you heard from them. "I sense you are quite passionate about your position . . ."
- If necessary, ask probing questions to get to the real issue.
- Don't get hooked. You don't have to tell them everything you know on the subject. Answer the question as best you can in a few sentences. If the rest of the room appears completely enthralled with the question, perhaps you can continue. If not, answer in a way that connects the question to the objective of your presentation.
- Suggest you get together later to continue the discussion. Finish by saying something along the lines of "Sally, you have asked an excellent question that will take longer than we have here to answer. How about we meet later or after the program and we can continue this conversation?" Then break eye contact and move to the next question.

QUESTIONS FROM THE FAR SIDE

If you get a question that doesn't relate to your topic, you have a couple of options for dealing with it:

- Answer the question briefly.
- Artfully tie the seemingly irrelevant question back to your topic.
- Ask, "Does anyone else here have a similar concern?" If the audience doesn't, answer the question very briefly and offer to speak with the participant after the presentation. If the audience does, well, then go where the audience wants to go!
- If the question is really wacko, just say, "That is not what we are here to discuss" and move on. Your audience will silently thank you.

LONG-WINDED ANSWERS

When a question becomes a long-winded speech, you must politely yet firmly interrupt the questioner and ask him to "ask the question, in the interest of saving time." Your audience will appreciate your ability to bring focus to the discussion.

If you have trouble with this, listen to National Public Radio's program *Talk of the Nation* or other talk shows to learn how serious professionals skillfully focus the discussion.

Bottom line: Be polite, calm, and courteous. Answer as best you can, balancing the time allotted, the personalities in the room, and your objectives.

Don't forget to check out more resources and downloads at www.boringtobravo.com.

CHAPTER SIX RECAP

Let's recap this chapter using a wide range of questioning techniques:

• Open-ended question: What is the most compelling insight you had while reading this chapter?

_____

• Situational question: During a presentation, have you ever been called on by a presenter when you didn't feel prepared?

_____

• Provocative question: What is the biggest concern you have about asking questions of the audience?

_____

• Rhetorical question: You don't really expect an answer to a rhetorical question, do you?

_____

• Take a poll: Have you ever confused your audience by asking a rhetorical question when you really were taking a poll, or vice versa?

_____

• Ask a series of enrolling questions: Do you currently ask questions during your presentations? Do they inspire conversation with the audience? Once they get talking, do you find you can't keep up with the energy in the room?

_____

• Encourage questions: How do you encourage questions from the audience?

_____

• Interview a participant: How and when are you going to interview a participant in your next presentation?

_____

• Closed question: Are you ready to move on to the next chapter on questions and answers, otherwise known as Q&A?

_____

ACTION PLAN

Based on the information in this chapter, I intend to

Continue _____

Start _____

Stop _____

www.ingramcontent.com/pod-product-compliance
Lightning Source LLC
Chambersburg PA
CBHW051354200326
41521CB00014B/2573